INVISIBLE HORSES

INVISIBLE HORSES

Rosalind Brackenbury

Hanging Loose Press
Brooklyn, New York

Published by Hanging Loose Press, 231 Wyckoff Street, Brooklyn, New York 11217-2208. All rights reserved. No part of this book may be reproduced without the publisher's written permission, except for brief quotations in reviews.

www.hangingloosepress.com

Printed in the United States of America
10 9 8 7 6 5 4 3 2 1

Hanging Loose Press thanks the Literature Program of the New York State Council on the Arts for a grant in support of the publication of this book.

Cover photograph: "Winter Horses" by Nicholas Bell, 9" x 9"

Cover design: Marie Carter

ISBN 978-1-934909-56-0

Library of Congress cataloging-in-publication available on request.

Acknowledgments: I would like to thank E.J.Miller-Laino and Galen Williams, early readers of many of these poems, for their encouragement and suggestions; also the Poetry Guild of Key West for support over many years; as well as my husband, Allen Meece, for his unfailing enthusiasm for my poems—and for being there at that poetry reading in 1992. To all at Hanging Loose Press, thanks for taking on another book of mine and making it such a beauty.

Some of these poems were published in *Hanging Loose*, and others in *Dicemos*, edited by J.D. Adler in Key West.

CONTENTS

I

II

III

IV

V

I

THE OLD POET

I remember him at eighty-nine
in his chair after lunch on his balcony
high above the ocean's fumble,

eyes closed, cap tipped, hands folded
over a blue sweatshirt,
apparently asleep;

but who knew, maybe writing
deep inside, because
the poems came, like birds visiting
whether he tried or not, it seemed.

They grew shorter that winter,
condensed, clear as a thumbprint,
as he went on practicing, daily,

for the last big one,
wings wide enough
to carry him out.

TUESDAY

It was the day the letters came,
the ones written by our mothers
to answer the ones we wrote
on Sundays—we had church, I played hockey,
I wrote an essay—the ones saying
nothing, not saying I miss you,
I want to be with you.

The words in my mother's letter—no,
let's start with the voice calling out
our surnames, leaving out
the ones with no letter—

at last her handwriting
on the envelope, the stamp
with the Queen on it, the young queen,
and the postmark, naming the place
I miss, and the way I snatch it up
from the tray

and walk quickly away
to slit it open in private
and read my name, and what they did
on Sunday, and how I wasn't there,
and yet they did it all without me—

walks, lunch, the dog, my brothers –
I can skip on to the end where she misses me.
She does miss me.

But if the letter isn't there,
if it hasn't come?
My day empties, rocks
like a bottle in water and is thrown back

on a bare shore.

Let's start with that impossibility,
so that it won't be what happens.
Let's admit we are
children, using magic to make love work,
let's take that bare simplicity:
a letter to stand in for all the rest.

THE COST

My daughter and I go to restaurants
to sit across from each other,
a white cloth between us
clean as a sun-dried sheet,
napkins, cutlery, everything
arranged just right; a waiter
brings the menu, the wine list,
asks her to taste, to choose.
I don't count the cost; it was
paid for long ago in all
the kitchens of our lives,
their mess and haste—the question
being always, what's for dinner?
In the rush and argument of family,
meals slapped down fast, voices raised.

It is the opposite of hand-to-mouth,
of barely held silences, and the way
women serve. The way she learned
from me to make just something,
anything, from what was in the fridge,
and dishes still to wash.
In restaurants, we take our time,
sip, talk. She chooses steak.
I watch her feed on luxury
the way I watched her decades ago
suck from bottles, milk going down
to clothe her tiny bones in flesh
enough to last.

AFTER THE SWIM

The Mediterranean dallies at our feet,
where we sit, old now, suits wet,
and salt dries on us in hot sun:

I think of the photograph, myself aged five
or so, pulling him, my younger brother, out
of the frilled wave of an English sea,
and can't remember

did I feel, big sister, responsible, and
so seized his hand to splash shoreward
in answer to some urgent call, or was it
sheer joy in the moment

that made me grab his fist and pull
so we ran together splashing
towards whoever took that photograph,
our grins wide,

our flapping cotton hats,
water-logged suits, to come
hurtling out of the water
into a future we couldn't guess at

but is this.

FRIENDS

Who are my friends? I ask, or wonder,
stepping into that playground without family,
cat or dog; no brothers here, no neighbors;
girls in checked dresses, blue and white—
they stare, I stare. My mother said,
you will make friends here; but who
are my friends, and who my enemies?

Behind the apple tree, I tie my invisible horse
to a branch and go forth into Friend Land.
Some girls flick their hair and sneer. Others
look scared. They have white socks,
they have sashes. They ask, who are you?
My name isn't enough.
One pokes me in my gingham chest,

another says, don't you know, we're not allowed
on the grass behind the tree, what were you doing
there? Tying up my horse, I say.
Your horse? What is its name?
She's dark, about my size, I saw her crying
when her mother left. I saw her stuff
in her pocket her hanky soaked with tears.

Silver King, I tell her. What's yours?
We canter off into friendship. Others follow.
It's like this with horses, you have one
then you have a herd, and their neighing
and tossing, their galloping, their flying manes
turn playground to open prairie,
everyone to rider, foe to friend.

MERINGUE

I rode Meringue on headlands, high
above the churning sea; we galloped
on cropped turf above kings' burial mounds
along the island's spine, where wind
carved trees and gorse
lit the gray land with its yellow flare.

Back in the yard,
he pushed to the trough, nose sunk
deep with the long suck of horses
at the watering hole.
I slid his saddle to the tree,
lifted the bridle off, and rinsed
the green-flecked bit,
pushed brushes on both hands to clean
his sweating neck, and led him out.

Meringue, his name—his color
edged from palest cream
to burnished white of egg. I sang
his name as I saw him
saunter from me into the field,
I breathed my own palms for his smell,
for the horse-sweat that grimed
all the life-lines and love-lines I had then;

I kept it as long as I could,
as lovers sniff up body scents,
wanting essences, stung to hope
by the whiff, the after-scent
of things I was too young to name—

Even young, you know
when love has reached
as far as it can and has to go,
free animal, back to its element.

He browsed the paddock's edge,
I called his name just once, Meringue;
and saw him lift his head
and turn away.

GOLD

We are in a jeweler's shop, he and I—
my son who has met me at the station—
and we are buying gold. My son buys gold
against the time in which there will be nothing,
in which it can be pawned for money, even food.
He says it holds its value. He believes in it
as he believes in religion and lighting candles
in front of suffering saints.
I am buying gold—these tiny drops like liquid
mercury, to hang from my own ears,
softer than silver, to last my lifetime.
I will never pawn them,
will wear them to remind me of this day
and of my son, and of believing in something
that will save us— not pawnshops, not gold,
but a way of loving what is, as it flies past.
Gold drops, tear drops, snow drops: nothing lasts,
not this moment in a shop, not the lunch we'll have
afterwards, not the promise of one thing ransomed
against another; just what flies between us, blows
in the sudden wind outside, lights up
our faces in the gold-glow.

Dorset: Rest & Be Thankful

I climb the steep hill
grassy to its summit's curve,
reach the land's spine,
walk among narrow stares of sheep

to the stone seat
where the carved words
Rest & Be Thankful
now blurred with age
and lichen, can't be read.

Here my parents used to sit
after the long climb,
she with her skirt tucked up,
feet in sensible shoes,
a scarf tying her hair;

he leaning forward
one elbow on his knee,
a hand on hers,
face to the wind and
blue gaze seaward.

I see them still, their pleasure
and relief. Their lookout
from the place they loved,
the words carved once
invisibly still written here.

To My Nieces

You girls—women now—remind me
in a glance of someone
I used to know:
my mother, my young self?

Where there was always
that male rub and push, brothers and father
around me like bullocks in a field;
now you are here to show
our tribe turning to the female:
you are black-haired, clear-eyed.
You speak to me of love affairs.

We drink coffee
together, we drink wine.
You ask my opinion.
You are dressed for the occasion,
in heels, in spangled dresses, in stark black.
In white satin. In tiny skirts.
You amaze me
with your beauty.

You are not my children
but my brothers' children, secrets
they carried in them all that time; yes,
they too awaited you;
yet inimitably yourselves—
the ones we wanted,
whom we all missed
without knowing you;
who now take on the complex world
to change it simply
by your presences.

WEDDING, BERLIN

In a part of the city that seemed hard to find
even in a taxi, it was like a dream of ruins:

we huddled waiting in the courtyard
for their arrival: the bride suddenly Victorian,
her nape swanlike, bending in white satin
to emerge from the small blue Trabbi
as if from a battered shell and pose against graffiti
her man like a bodyguard at her unfamiliar skirts.
Her friends were in cocktail dresses, strappy
on cold shoulders in October wind; three
sisters, eyes black with mascara,
strode in heels across cobbles
through a shattered arch.

All the young men were in evening dress,
with sneakers; most were bald.
And up the dusty stairs we went one by one,
clutching up skirts, careful on heels
to where candles flickered on long tables
set for a feast and music played.
It was a wedding in part
of the once-split city come together
across blitzed walls, fallen watch-towers,
all the old history; where museums
of oppression take tickets and lure you in.
Here, pure, almost seamless, a streaming together:
speeches in German, English, Spanish, chat
in Arabic, the music borderless, as everybody
took everybody else in their arms
and the wedding dance began.

Bear-night

for Allen

What have you needed, I wonder
as you write from your birthplace,
the dark woods of Kentucky
where you are camping alone
in a small tent,
where there are bears, you say;
they come to snatch food from campers, they rear up
in the night massive and shaggy as nightmare,
to rend tents with their claws. What do you
need to find in this wilderness, in this dark,
in among ancient tombs—your great grandfather's
grave on a rocky hilltop, wild man excluded
for all eternity from the smooth green lawn
where the good Baptists lie? What sends you
if not your own blood, your own memory,
pre-birth even, of the men who preceded you
carving their way west, stumbling into America,
pushing on at last through the mountains
they had not expected? Maybe, husband,
you need your woods, your campfire
against the darkness where there are bears;
your loneliness;
maybe you will come back to me
lighter of some ancient weight
out of the bear-night, to meet me again,
clear of what it was
that hunted you.

MATTHEW ON THE CHAMPS ELYSÉES

Where Napoleon marched his Grande Armée
and recently, a puffed-up president,
unnaturally blond, lifted an ageing profile for the press;
where pomp and luxury go hand-in-hand:
Vuitton, Cartier, Armani
flanking the avenues of commerce
and military pride,

a small boy on a scooter, hair to the breeze,
bare-kneed between shoppers,
browsers, tourists from Japan,
skirting the nuns, the selfie-takers,
all the traffic of the afternoon,
swoops, turns on a dime, and hurtles back,
the sidewalks of the famous
for this six-year-old, his personal race track

and stops, sudden as if braked,
and runs, arms windmilling as if to try
flying next, to where we wait,
staid adults at the bus stop, and the parade
goes on, insists on past victory and present state
while he carves his swerving anarchic way,
bird on the future's wing.

II

SOLSTICE 2016

for Ann

My old friend died at the Solstice—
sun stopped, dawn a winter light—

She was in her own room, son and daughter
one each side, holding her hands, singing,
sometimes weeping.
Her old cat slept at her feet.

I imagine it: the cat winking, shoulders pulled up
under ruff of fur, edging heavy up the bed as cats do
to push, knead, purr.

I don't know what's it's like to take
a last breath. To depart—if that's what
we do. To start a new day
motherless, this I know.

Ann's old cat, wide-eyed in the morning,
leaps off to clatter a bowl for food
on the kitchen floor.

I imagine the cat—Booska—going down
to the emptied kitchen.
The rest—no, I can't go there:
each death is tailored to a life,
one person's shadow
itself alone.

HEDGEHOG

"Mrs. Tiggy-Winkle was . . . only a Hedgehog," Beatrix Potter, "The Tale of Mrs. Tiggy-Winkle."

For Billy Collins (with thanks to Philip Larkin and Beatrix Potter)*

Once, we English loved our small wild animals—
the hedgehog, sooty nose and clever eyes,
the badgers who played in moonlight in some dell.

We had dells then, we had woodland,
and used to put saucers out with bread and milk
to feed our hedgehog, marvel that she came
like Santa in the night, to sup her fill.

We supped fills in those far-off days;
we had Mrs. Tiggy-Winkle, cozy
in cap and apron, making tea.

We were an innocent lot, crazy perhaps
but not murderous. We suffered
when we killed, or so we said –
viz. Larkin with his mower, agonized.

And at the book's end, when Mrs. Tiggy
shockingly naked of cap and gown,
a simple animal, was seen
to scuttle to the far woods on all fours,

We felt we had been stripped back
with her to anonymity, even barbarism:
a feral commonplace, with fleas.

*   The poet Philip Larkin once killed a hedgehog with his lawnmower and was mortified, as he fed hedgehogs bread and milk every night. The poet Billy Collins asked me why I thought he did this. When I was young, I said, this is what English people did.

VISITOR

I'm eating breakfast,
yoghurt and granola, with a pear,
my wickedly dark
Cuban coffee
hissing into the cup

when I see these two eyes
like peppercorns
a lozenge-shaped head
a wrinkled old-man's neck
and yellow-patterned shell
and the turtle comes out of the grass
and looks up at me.

I offer a lettuce-leaf;
he chews half-moons in it.
I say, hello, and who are you?
Something about the way
he turns his head

reminds me of an old poet
I once knew. I hesitate
to ask him, are you he?
Then a helicopter rushes
overhead, spraying to kill
the mosquito larvae
that breed dengue fever
in these parts.

My visitor
looks up, eyeing
the predator, trundles
into the liriope grass
that hides him
from air attack

so I never am sure
who he is or why he's come to me
except to say, write a poem,
get it down, now; everything
is a poem
including this.

Sign Language

for J. T.

Since I saw you last,
since your one good hand came out
to grip mine; since I saw in your face
the urgency of words

and since I groped for them,
in the space between your fingers,
such a small space—
one finger for yes, two for no,
a horizontal hand for, let me pause;
a fist shaken, got it wrong,
and all the letters of the alphabet
become the shapes you make in air;

since I embarked with you
on this difficult journey—
silence, interruption,
the blurts of the body, the firm gaze of the eye—
since your hand moved in to stand for everything:
the sounds that are human,
too easily had, that can betray us;

since we began on this other language,
you the expert, I the translator
stumbling after, I've learned your way slowly,
friend, and will follow you
into the realms you live in now,
to grasp your emphatic
orthography, as best I can. Poetry,
the shortest distance always
between two humans.
Your poem, one finger at a time.

Poetry Reading at Shakespeare & Company on The Day after "Brexit."

For Sam Hamill and Salah al-Hamdani

The American poet says his country's government
is a terrorist organization.
The Iraqi poet says
his country has been seized by pirates.

One was imprisoned in California,
the other in Abu Ghraib.

Today my old country, England, shames me.
I reach in my mind for the green hills,
the honeysuckle and roses of the garden
that was my parents': for my brother, my son,
my friends, shamed in their turn
not by violence but by mediocrity.

I have to remember the poetry, the dawn chorus
of my youth, as the American poet remembers
the light on the sides of the Canyon de Chelly,
as the Iraqi goes back in his mind
to the lost gardens of Baghdad.

We lose our mothers, our gardens, our faith
in history; we remember our rivers,
the Euphrates, the Rio Grande,
the stripling Thames under its willows.
Our childhoods.

Something is not lost.
Something is never quite lost.

POETRY

It starts small: a bud, a leaf, a bird.
This particular small brown Cuban wagtail (I think)
that hops on stick legs after crumbs
and will fly through the kitchen
and out again.

Sometimes it expands and takes you with it:
the migrations are spectacular
like dreams you couldn't make up if you tried –
like last night's dream in which
I led my parents

into a hotel room to make me
and told them, "I'm glad you could
get together" as I left them there.

Sometimes a life grows
seventy years or more.

Sometimes, it stays small. They touch
and nothing comes of it.
The bird hops clean away.

FAILURE

*("Last night as I lay sleeping/ I dreamed—marvelous
error—that I had a beehive here inside my heart and the
golden bees/ were making white combs and sweet honey
from my old failures."*
      —Antonio Machado, translated by Robert Bly.)

I read you, Antonio Machado,

sitting out here with my coffee,
trying not to listen to the noises of the day –
shriek of wood-saw, blurt of traffic
on wet streets—

and think about your golden bees
making white combs and sweet honey
from your old failures—
and so, presumably, mine.

Yesterday's rejection letter came:
'we all loved it but unfortunately . . . '
and now you remind me, sleep is
a gathering of bees,

dream is renewal, even an idle
breakfast stretching into the morning
can hold a hidden reconfiguring
of sorts;

that it's all going on out of sight
as my neighbor invisibly mows his grass
and someone deafens the street
with a leaf-blower;

that not-doing is possibly
our purpose, while the beehive
thrums in the heart; that poets
will always be read

if we write about
failure, the topic nobody mentions,
except in whispers,
except among bees.

THE POET'S HOLIDAY

She'd rather prune the hedge
or even scrub the floor;
polish windows
with balled-up newspaper
or even rinse sheets
in the tub—

She's here to write,
or so she'd planned,
to be alone, to let words
tumble on to the page,
justifying absence.

Now, she'd rather pour wine
at lunchtime, pick up a book—
someone else's—eat cheese
and strawberries in her fingers,
listen to the radio
do the crossword,

watch the squirrel run on the wire
and let him be just a squirrel,
let him go free;
not record the doe
met in the wet woods yesterday—

not make anything of her
nor of that meeting,
not invent some fellow-feeling or exchange;
to let the world be—trees,
stone, earth, animal—not to address
another, a beloved, or say
that he is missed—

not to try for a phrase,
an image that will say it all: perhaps
just to lie back, watch the blue space
made between clouds that pass,
draw close, and part.

ODE TO THE FRENCH LANGUAGE

You taught me *chou* for "cabbage"—at five
we giggled and counted—*treize, quatorze, quinze,*
read about *une souris qui mangeait*
des bougies—and her naughty children,
les enfants de Madame Souris;

then I heard my father, driving too fast,
called *salaud*!
such a word!
such hiss, such insult—
what did it mean?

And when you slipped inside me at last
at eighteen,
one astonishing word
and phrase at a time,
to spread like mercury,
inhabit me,

I welcomed you like a lover,
ah, *amour*—words
of seduction, grace, pleasure;
danced with you through the years
glancing sideways to glimpse
my fluent double

who doesn't sound like me
yet speaks from my mouth, witty even,
slangy, and angry, and in love
and subtle as water;
who flags when I'm tired,
revives after wine;

I carry you inside me,
brimming: there's a spillage
sometimes, a stumbling,
a loss of balance, then a precise
righting of this other self,

a moving back in tune. You have
a softness in you I need, and
an exactness too, like dance steps,
grammar like a hand at my back
to straighten my spine,
vowels to shape my lips, my tongue;
you change me, you allow change,
you purse me up and shake me out,
open and use my hands, loosen me
and draw me up. I am, for this time
your creation, I learn you like
flying, like launching,

while my parental English
stands apart,
and lets you take me, make me
what you will.

III

MEMORIES OF HARRY IN KEY WEST

Why do I think first
of your beautiful shirts?
Like Gatsby's, enough to make one cry.
And your voice, with its surprising
gentleness, asking, how am I?
Guessing when things weren't easy.
Your exact and generous prose,
and the way you wrote blurbs, so
carefully, as if they were poems;
poems as if they were puzzles,
stories that were recipes,
novels that were lists. I think
of your vast intelligence,
often held in check: the space
left in our world without it;
of your Olympian grace
* —aristocratic, yes, yet thoroughly*
and still American, leaving out
small talk, cutting to the chase.
The pink champagne you ordered
for my birthday that year;
that sense you gave of sure festivity.
I think of your brave last battles, your grimace
of pain, half-joking—"This part
of life's not fun." And how,
faced with the end, you remained so much
a gent. I guessed, you'd had
a plenitude of fun: in life,
in literature, in love, the best; and now,
I like to imagine you pain-free, alive,
with glass in hand, at ease to chat with old
lost friends upon some Oulipian cloud,
where no unwanted vowels may intrude
and all the saddest stories end in jest.

THE GREAT BEAUTY

Maybe all we need to hear is:
look around. Slow to a calmer pace,
sit on a wall in the morning
as the people pass.

Watch the trees' change:
gumbo limbo sheds old leaves,
grows new, without pause,
mahogany looses its pale showers,
poinciana starts up its
slow-burning fires,
just as the new green comes in

and wind today moves everything about—
flowers, water, leaves, grass.

Look—give up busyness for a season,
spend your days stunned and wordless
in the great beauty:
mockingbirds sing daylong,
the woodpecker drills posts early,
the ocean flashes at your gates,
hawks hang in the blue.

HIDDEN

1.

Rain in the night.
under a single sheet
we turn, hear thunder, sleep
again.
Ballet of bare limbs in the dark;
morning: two lizards fuck on the stone slab.

2.

Wind moves the massed leaves,
wind that turned in the night,
comes in from the west. A cooler caress,
no sweat.
How the human animal craves comfort,
how the wind comes in from everywhere,
crosses our island like the breath of the world.

3.

Over breakfast we talk of hidden things,
the ones we'd never tell a soul.
I listen, wonder what you hide
and if you will ever tell me.

The Taste of This World

Peach

Today I bought a sheep's cheese in the market,
a melon—ripe for today—some ham,
a yellow peach. Jazz on the radio,
and though the sky above Paris is gray
and none of you, my loves, is here,
I taste the cream inside the whitish crust,
bite into pink-stained peach flesh
and have to say, even before I brew my coffee,
that here I sit alone
riotous with gratitude.

Buying Cherries In Chinatown

They are so fat and red, I can't resist;
so clutch my plastic bagful to be weighed,
among the Chinese women on Saturday,
their cuts of meat, their root-bundles
bound for tonight's table,
and the dollars in flipped bills
changing hands fast as a poker game.
I fumble with notes and coins while
a sort of click of maybe sympathy—
she isn't from here—sounds around me.
Not part of the rich and necessary
ritual, not buying for my family
or weighing a bargain,
I go out alone with my harvest
to begin eating them one after another
like a solitary child, split flesh with
my tongue to feel the juice, and spit
rude stones in secret on the street.

Teaching the Tongue

I've read that what you eat with
changes the taste. A heavy spoon
makes custard creamier. Cheese
eaten off a knife tastes saltier.

Sitting here eating cherries
from a porcelain bowl
I taste their fatness from thin china.

We all knew it but ignored it—
the container and the implement,
outer and inner, bowl and spoon.
Bowl fits hands, spoon
the curl of tongue.

To be fed with a silver spoon
teaches the tongue to lick.
To drink from a tin cup
aches like water
too cold to swallow.

CARRO, PROVENCE

For André and Roseline

1. White Cat

Pigeons call through my dreams
and in the night the wind gets up
to creak about the house.
Outside, the pines sigh like the sea
and early, light comes through
the scrim of them. A white cat
thinking she's unseen, comes
to rip at the garbage bag for bones,
then goes to lick her paws
under the hedge.
My dream was of flying;
I only had to breathe in hard
and flap my arms, and soar.
What was the cat's dream?
Gristle, marrow, juice on a licked paw.

2. Pines

Folded in the white hammock stretched
between two pine trunks' blistered skin,
on this last afternoon I lie
like a fish in a sandwich, and gaze up.
From here, trees topple, they spread
against the sky like open umbrellas,
their cones cluster and may fall;
the smell of resin, the chant of wind—
Aeolian music; surely the trees
themselves are singing, singing
in celebration of the wildness

that shakes and releases
cones, pine needles,
seeds of the coming year.

3. "O Sole Mio"

Full moon this week and the season shifts,
you can feel it—darkness at morning, cloud,
then the apricot light, wind across water,
the shiver of it in the trees, a chill you waited for,
almost wanted. The beach, when you go down
the familiar summer path, through pine woods,
past fig and oleander, is nearly empty now—
just two swimmers and a group playing
beach volley ball without a net.

The trees have moved all night, sighing in the wind—
mistral or tramontane—and on the far side,
beyond the Sunday fish market,
dozens of windsurfers crouch on their frail boards
under the bucking sails, slice across waves,
rise, fall, rise again, as the white breakers
land on the shore, and withdraw, and begin
again, and something in you wants to slide up,
fall away, begin again—or sing. Or shout —
so that later when the fat man enters the water
in the blue bay where it's calm still,
wind only patterning the sea's face;
when he opens his arms wide and his lungs like an opera star,
and sings out so grandly 'O Sole Mio' before
he dives—you clap, and the volleyball players
clap, and you all cheer as he comes up sudden
and bald as a walrus; the last swimmer,
singing out this summer to its end.

Threshold, at Les Patrières

Small black dragonflies with startling blue
bodies flit above nettles; I think
they are butterflies till I come close
and see the electric blue tubes,
the hectic wings. Better to be
surprised, even mystified, than to see what you
expect to see—yes, and the black bee
deep in the confused pink heart of the flower,
the bean that plummets to earth
from a high branch, bent as a
boomerang, flies like a summer bat.
The unknown bird that calls all day with its question
and the tentative mouse-scrabble at night
that half-wakes me; the small brown cat
with amber eyes who visits, pauses
on the threshold, won't quite come in.

IV

CHEZ PAUL

Here's the gilt mirror showing me
myself, almost as if I belonged here.
Here's the chair you sit in, green velvet,
and the blue-painted buffet
and there the portraits,
the Modigliani women
you love and imagine.
And you're not here, but your voice,
cracking a little with age,
your presence, slower now,
your old jacket on the chair back, your books—
this is how we change the world,
I see, simply by our presence in it.
By our absences.

GLOBAL POSITIONING

"Pre-literate societies did not have maps"

The maps are vanishing: the ones I grew up with,
the world in Mercator's Projection—
America dangling on the left, Australia
far below, little England sticking a toe
into the Atlantic, and the pink
stain of empire across continents;
the atlas, the bright globe, the maps
we drew or traced in Geography,
crayoning the seas' blue edge.
Old maps, wavering coastlines, gaps
and "Here be dragons";
Ordnance Survey, to be folded,
taken on walks in a backpack
with chocolate and an apple in the English rain.

The N7 going south, the Michelin map of France
across my knees on the long drive
to the sun. The D-roads, thin yellow
veins between villages, curled
around farmsteads, fields: tracks
of a horse-drawn age. Maps spread on the floors
of foreign rooms, promising the whole journey.
Now, I miss crooked roads, hairline rivers,
churches marked with a cross,
the molehill rings of topography;
Now, we have a line from A to B,
a voice that tells us not to deviate:
the route is set.
The maps have vanished
that showed us not only where we were,
but who, in reading them,
we might become.

Ocean Beach

for Robin O.

We wanted, we said, to come to an edge
and here we are, a continent at our backs,
facing west to a dim horizon

where the bus left us, its last passengers,
where the roiling gray Pacific
flicks spray up spattered rocks,

and far down on the sand
tiny people race their tiny dogs
against its spreading arcs —
such space, such wind and light
you want to run, or embrace, or fly
into the air with pelicans and gulls

where few people walk under the ancient trees,
where cypress, pine and monkey puzzle
stretch their trunks skyward over time

and the marks of human effort are
simply scattered, in ruins, in roses on gray stone,
in arum lilies and geraniums

and this is it, we say, the land's end,
the vastness no one can fill.

SECRET BEACH, MAY

The clouds of May have their linings
as they balloon up over the sea.
Everything has its center:
the sticky buds of the sea-grape
turn to stiff red leaves that sprout
within the green, still tacky
to the touch, like paint that hasn't
yet had time to dry.

The sand has its clean rim still
as the tide retreats. Before
the jet-skis' scream, before
fishing boats going out
before the first footprint,
the silence: like listening
to your own blood, like memory
before entry into the noisy world,
things ripening unseen.

THE RIVER CREUSE

This summer's rain has filled and overflowed
its banks; today it is high, fast-moving,
tea-brown, and as I come down to walk beside it
I close my eyes to listen to its voice —
more than a ripple, less than a roar, a cluck
or chuckle, no breath in and out like the ocean,
no pause, but on and on, changeless, more so
perhaps than anything in life,

it chants its quiet perpetual song; it's why
I walk here, river to one side of me, nut and ash
grown tall now on the other, and the stone wall
capped with moss, the grass thick, damp,
green after weeks of rain. I come to find
the river moving behind its scrim of trees, its glitter
of sun on brown, as I have for over thirty years,
and each time different.

Once, I pushed a canoe out into rapids, paddled fast
upstream, moored beside willows to swim
in its brown backwaters; once, sat
on a rock and felt its tug at my waist.
Once, with my new husband, paddled downstream
in a green canoe to the next village, past
cliffs and islands, places where the river
parted like hair for braiding and met again.

Postcards from Dorset

1.

I could tell you
how the rain slides sideways
like theatre scenery,
the scrim of it
masking the pine wood

or how the blue tits hang
from wet twigs,
acrobats after berries,
how chaffinches dart
in the hedge;

how nobody comes, or speaks
but the trees thrash like ships
in a wild sea.

How even the men working next door
have packed up and gone
from where they joked over tea
and sandwiches
in yesterday's sun;

and that in that sun
I walked up the ancient hill
to sit on its summit
and look both ways,
over sea and land.

I could tell you how I walk
the same paths, and how, over decades
little has changed

only the old trees growing
and thickening,

only I, in my life span,
in my same skin, walking on.

2.

I am now the age of my grandmother,
who watched me at ten, at eleven
hurry up the peat track to this same hill.
Heather roots and wet bracken tug
at my boots as they did my childish
sandals, feet knowing the way.

What does it mean, to age?
I see her motionless at the window,
looking out, or slowly walking
to post a letter, stick in hand.
She was old, it was a given;
we ran on ahead.

The stone church here has stood
a thousand years. I sat
beside her in the wooden pew;
then she was gone. I lived.
The oak, the cedar, the Scots pine
will outlive me.

When I go, it will be just life,
I think. A tree falls, another grows.
This evening, after rain, sun spreads
over the white cliffs, the shifting sea.

Spinning, Key West

Today's kettle of turkey vultures
black on blue, wheels high;
everything's shining—palm leaves,
grass, the small buds of orchids.
The spider's at it, spanning the void
between laundry line and outstretched leaf,
her dense red body making and remaking
the world, one thread at a time,
saliva-bright, hair-thin.

A new morning after winter:
we all want to start again,
spinning, budding, shining,
reaching to span whatever distance we can.
To know it's possible. To dare it
over and over, whatever the outcome,
whoever may blunder into our own
frail constructions, make us
start again.

SUNDAY, PARIS

Today heat pours
between buildings. On the square,
the musicians played, the dancers danced,
all of them grown older; oranges
from Spain tumbled on the market stalls,
the melons ripened, figs grew soft.

Sirens in mid-afternoon, and then
everyone went home to eat or sleep:
I'm here with the window open,
last year's geraniums dry on the window rail,
a stillness where loneliness could
root, like the dried grass

that hangs from the gutter outside
my window in the silent yard—or,
its kinder twin, poetry, begin
its solitary consoling whisper
if I can listen, and not miss
the telephone, other Sundays, you.

ODE TO A PARISIAN POPLAR

> *"Passant, regarde ce grand arbre . . . "*
> —Yves Bonnefoy

You and the wind; you and that invisible other—
you capture my eyes as I sit at my window,
at my table, as I try to write, as I eat; as I lie
on the white sofa mid-afternoon,
nothing moving anywhere but the fan's air
and the slight hot breath that moves your topmost
twigs like the end of a cat's tail twitching.
You poplar, you shimmer and shift,
shape-changer, green angel, country lover
in the heart of the city, sentinel
between buildings here in the packed streets
of the *cinquième*; you stand between me
and the next building where the light
burns nightlong on the top floor and solitary
smokers lean from windows.
When I returned exhausted from
the Camino, I watched you, I did little else;
sipped mineral water and watched you;
fresh from the wild forests of Galicia,
I needed you like air, like water, like space and silence.
In the heat of Parisian summers
when the sky is beaten like metal and the air
scrapes the throat, I greet you, watch you change, move, breathe,
create waves in your branches, spin
poems from your small twig ends,
carve out green hollows of the imagination.
Because I have never seen your trunk, don't
know where your roots grow, because you
float like a cloud above rooftops
I can imagine your green
childhood, see you grow from one solitary

seed in this place, to the tree you are,
growing and growing beyond me in your
reach for the heights of sky.

5 A.M. POEM

The room's already pale with dawn.
No traffic on the street.
Here in the wide bed with the linen sheet
we bought together one year in the flea market
liking its heft and rough old touch, I miss
your warm left hand in mine;
my right hand feels for you across
the bed and the night hours, wanting
that male width and firmness to tell me
of conscious presence, then of sleep;
but you're in your country and I, wakeful—
in my country of the mind,
knowing what poets must do—
reach for tisane, a pen,
a yellow legal pad instead, and begin
to unravel what hurts, what I'm here for,
what is still so generously given.

Pascal, on rue Pascal

He said it, *le grand philosophe*,
that all our ills come from
not being able to sit still
in a room.

Here I sit, in my room, on the street
named for him and his philosophy.
Un savant. Are there savants among us
still?

Nothing moves. The geraniums on the sill
dry out; in here these walls
hold me, and all my energy
and the activity—

the shops, museums, parks,
the great river itself, its traffic,
the city in its turmoil, groups of soldiers,
people in cafés, the flow
of fountains, the photographs, flashes,

poses, videos, and the boats on the pond
in the gardens, Paris, the endless parade of it,
sirens and songs, the homeless with no room
to go to, the boy in the gutter with the squeezebox,
the scarved women at the *boulangerie* door—

all outside. I, in my room, rue Pascal,
not going out and nearly mad with it,
on the philosopher's street

in the eye of the savant, who knew
what he was saying, and that it was
never easy, nor would be.

SPIRALS, LES PATRIÈRES

I come down to the river
and the gray heron fishing at the bank
rises up to depart.

Back at the house in the hot yard
the yard of pink hollyhocks,
black bees busy at their hearts,

I look up to see the buzzard rise
on spirals of invisible currents,
higher and higher, pulling my gaze

up taut as he circles, planes,
turns, black cinder in the blue
and I am tugged upward

to spy the white bands on
his vanishing wings, to be sure
of what I've seen

before I have to leave this place,
try to write it, word by word,
never quite saying what it was.

VIRGINIA

We are giving up table napkins
and having coffee after dinner,
you wrote after moving to Bloomsbury
we are beginning on our decadent evenings.
It's heaven—like the Renaissance, you said
as the rude youth of Cambridge—
Lytton, Maynard, Clive—
lounged on your Turkey carpets, holding forth.

Later, Duncan and Roger Fry.
You talked of sex and postimpressionism
and who was in love with whom.
You had got rid of the furniture.
Tongues wagged. Yes, they are Leslie Stephen's
daughters, too bad how they turned out,
if only their poor mother were alive.

I picture you at twenty, hugging your knees
as the boys talked of buggery and books
and the world opened—as it does,
only to close again. Too soon, your darling
Thoby died. You swore he was living still,
that he took soup, even
a mutton chop. His temperature
was down, he would be well by Christmas.

You conjured the magic words, but
nothing, even your keenest of imaginations
worked, to bring back the dead.
It never would.
To save yourself
was already beyond you.

PAULA MODERSOHN BECKER

She had no name of her own, really—
just Paula.

What I find hard to bear,
stumbling out of the exhibition—all those rich canvases,
once she'd given up cardboard and muddy paints
and gloried in Paris and her oils—
was that she died so young.

Thirty-one, felled as if by lightning—
an embolism, from lying too still
after the huge event of childbirth —
didn't they know she was an artist,
that she painted those women's bodies
curled naked against their thriving fat babies,
blood running, milk at the ready,

women nobody could have stifled
under the tight sheet of conformity?

Didn't they know, from those bony little girls
each clutching a solitary flower,
each one a serious dreamer doomed to fail?

I think of the Sundays in Paris
when she couldn't stop painting
long enough even to have lunch,

when the paint burned in her mind, dripped
on to her canvases, when the brush
cramped her hand, and time ran out.

SHIPWRECK

This year, the Mediterranean sea
has shown its other face.

This year the drowned are just around the corner:
the ones without life jackets, the young, the old,
the babies, the small children.

This year this sea
is no playground.

Its currents catch and take.
Everything goes down—

rubber, plastic, wood,
shoes, toys,
caught among fish and weed.

I walk by this same sea,
my footprints clear
then gone. There's no one here

at dawn or evening
when the sun goes behind the mountain.
Only know it, be sure—

Down the coast they are landing,
they are coming ashore.
Some are carried.

Some lie beached like stranded jellyfish,
won't move again.

Who will forget the child
who lies face down, small
limbs rocked on the wave's edge?

This year we have to feel the shock of it.
The moored yacht in the bay
can't stay at anchor;

sailors out on the silk of afternoon
who spy an arm raised must go to haul
one more tired human in across the transom—
no common language
just an arm around the shoulders,
a hot drink, dry towel.

Go down to the summer sea:
scan the horizon,

this is the place
of shipwrecks.

We share what happens here.

CHRISTMAS

for John and Carol

After the calls to distant family—
heat wave in Australia, snowstorms
in Scotland—we come together,
all of us far from family, yet home
upon this fractured spit of land
where water rises closer every year
and the salt ponds spread.

This year we have become conspiracy:
we raise our glasses, speak aloud,
breathe upon freedom as on a small flame.
The sun goes down early. Light spreads
low across the ponds, where water laps
almost to our feet.

You have put down topsoil,
laid out mulch: it is what you do
as the islands shrink and the sea comes in
with the full moon. It is where we are,
where we sit, drink good wine, eat, talk,
glance sometimes over our shoulders,
shift our chairs a little closer in.

BODYWORK

I don't know where it goes from here.
I hurt; I am a bundle of bones on a table,
broken apart and then put back together,
the awkward mass of me clenched
in a grip that's pain and then release.
Nothing works. Hips out of joint,
I am dislocated, that is
put out of place; my coherence
cracked, as if I have gone up
to the ceiling to look down
on something too hard to live through,
birth maybe, maybe even death.
We can shatter, I learn, and then
be mended. We come back.
For the moment,
we do come back.

FLYING TO MEXICO

I relish the moment when we lift
into the blue—
through clouds, into a purity
no one could have guessed at till
this easy gift of flight—

the gasp, even silent, as the giant machine
soars through and out
across the Gulf

and we emerge, leave all
our past behind:
its shrunken clothes,
shoes bent out of shape,
old fears and aspirations;

we fly, we're on our way,
and if the thought enters
quick as a flicked knife,
you can die—it happens,
planes fall from the sky,
people are smashed to bits
to lie spread across countries
they'd never dreamed of visiting—

I know now I'd go down
seeing only this
absolute blue, deep
as all our imagined heavens,
the parts of me blown apart, yes,
but still, my soul,
the blue.

MARKET

I walk to the Thursday market—
tents set up, stalls under the trees
for the cheese-lady, the nut-man,
the organic tomatoes; the young
Ukrainians wash my hands
for me with Dead Sea salt
and the group at the bandstand,
singer in a pink hat, play Joni;
and the Indian silk skirts
flutter, the ceviche is handed out
in little plastic tubs, with plantains
on the side. You can taste honey,
try on a sun hat, buy chutney,
meet friends at the cheese stall,
talk politics, or this week's movies,
or that article in the *New Yorker*;
take a sliver of parmesan
to try. The pink flowers
fly from the tree whose name I never can
remember—like a wedding,
like a blessing, and the sky
between forked branches, April blue.

Yet still that other market's in my mind,
The one where the black flakes of ash
rise from the burned tents: or was it
a wedding, someone's coming of age,
were there cakes made, was rice offered,
was there saffron, and honey too
before the bird of death came down?
And will I ever be able again to visit
just this market, just the one I'm at today
with people harmlessly coming,
going, with their bags and baskets,

their bicycles and carts, their babies,
greeting, tasting, looking
at the sky from which no harm
comes, not yet, maybe not ever,
but where still you have to hear the music
telling you, it's how it is, from now on:
"both sides, both sides now."

Today, a Hummingbird

Today at breakfast, a hummingbird
visited the mimosa.
Febrile, tiny; a fast pulse
there—then gone.

Already helicopters
hover; knocks shake the doors
of sleepers. You wake:
The ICE patrol car's in the street.

Planes leave in the dark
for Haiti, Cuba, Guatemala,
Honduras. Look,

stick this inside your door:
the alert in three languages,
English, Spanish, Creole,

to tell you as you stumble out:
don't open the door.
You do not have
to answer.

Ask only
for the judge's
warrant. (There won't be one.)

If you open the door—
(Ah, where is the hummingbird
gone?—)

say goodbye,
to your children, your husband,
your wife. To your life here.

To the heart beat
in the mimosa at breakfast.
To the blameless blue sky
of yesterday.

JARDIN DES PLANTES

Morning, and at the menagerie the small kids cluster.
The wallabies are sitting under the water-spray,
their fur matted and wet. It's hot, even for marsupials.
A little boy says "Lapin!" and his teacher tells him,
no, not a rabbit but a kind of kangaroo. The child
repeats "Lapin!" until all the children are saying it,
Lapin! Lapin! And the young teacher smiles at me, shrugs.
Too hot to argue.

Two by two, the children in their school pinafores
with their lunch bags for a picnic, and their young teachers
who will hand them back to their parents at the day's end.
Two by two, holding hands, at the little zoo and
at each flowering plant and ancient tree,
at the bees' hotel, the meteorites, the whale skeleton,
the Carousel.

I can't help thinking of the others, babies like these,
locked up this summer in cages in the country I live in:
in Texas, in Arizona: no picnics, zoo, flowers, no
bee hotel, no laughing young teachers—
just bars for the children of Central America,
a hard floor, and no mama, no papa. No hugs
at the day's end. Not today, not tomorrow,
maybe not ever.

LIVING SPACE

Yesterday the hermit moved back
to his living space under the sea-grape
above the water's green chop.
I saw his bicycle, his striped umbrella,
his pack of provisions.

The osprey was not yet back in her nest
on the high pole. Five shrimp boats,
nets furled, headed in from the Gulf
making for port from the storm.
I sat on my rock, watching

and thought about space for living
and what we need from it, each one of us,
and about its architecture—
the green cave under the sea-grape,
the size of just one person—
and the way the light comes in.

Today the light glinted on green water
and the wind drove currents and
sargasso weed. Two people embraced
in the wave, needing only that space.

In the end, the living space is inside us,
between the bones of the skull, free
inside the chambers of the heart.
We inhabit it a little while and when we leave it,
who moves in? Where have we moved to?

PLACE DE CONTRESCARPE 2016

The trees are grown that were small when we were here
a quarter-century ago.
This evening at the same bar, I sit alone with *kir*
at a small round table, and see
the light change, creep up buildings as
the young musicians play jazz:
a barefoot drummer, bassist, sax,
the flautist prancing like the faun in the gardens.

I see how all little girls skip and sway
to the music, even as mothers tug them on,
and how the four soldiers strolling by
with submachine guns cocked, even younger
perhaps than the jazz men, can't risk a glance
or pause. We're getting used to them,

are almost glad they're here to make it safe,
this life of jazz, cafés, *kir*, dancing toddlers,
young women sure and sexy in heels and tiny skirts,
a man weaving through on his bike with groceries—
the old, the young, the babies, the couples
safe for now on the warm September square—

all is as it was, except today
it feels fragile, and even brave, to be out here,
out in all the cafés and squares of Paris:
the pregnant woman in the orange mini
who bends to place a coin in the hat, her child
dancing beside her in silver sandals:

all the beauty and all the pleasure
and the sky clear over rooftops and the trees
around the fountain putting down more roots;
and I think, if it's going to happen, let it be here,

as I sit at this small table, with jazz,
in the gold light of one more September evening—
it's not bravery, just the laziness of age.

But no, please, not for this baby only just starting
on her one life. Not for her. Not her
in her white dress, in her silver shoes,
jumping up and down to the music.

FIGS, MARSEILLE

(for Geneviève L.)

From her garden, she says,
offering them,
picked this morning
for our lunch—

their blue bloom
their intricate seeded
inner flesh.

A day later,
two on a white plate
show stretch marks,
sweat a little, ooze
their juice.

We eat them like memory,
end of summer
evening *entre chien et loup* —
their slight deliquescence.

As light abandons the far hills,
settles like paint on rooftops,

we taste the last figs, this season's bruised
epiphanies.

FOR EDITH

I can't imagine now
not setting out to catch the bus—the 83,
they don't go often, so I run—that takes me
past the Closerie, down rue d'Assas
to the stop at Cherche-Midi
where I walk fast past closed shops, carrying
flowers, a book, a bottle, to your door.

I punch the flickering numbers of the code,
the door swings open to the inside hall,
there's the intercom
and the glass elevator edged in brass
that lifts me to the fourth floor,
to the door with the dragon on it

that stands a little open, and to you.
Turbaned, in silk, you kiss me twice,
and take me in past Chagall and Ans Hey;
among roses and peonies, you tell me
to open the bottle, find the glasses—
"tu connais la maison"—

I clear a space on your table
and pour the wine—red, a good Bordeaux –
and you lean back and raise
your glass—"A nous." We begin
again. I can't imagine not doing this.
I don't want to imagine.
I want to pin you here
and tell whoever's listening, it was
like this, and this—sushi delivered,
the man paid, the light changing,
swallows diving at your window.

*

When Ans died in Amsterdam on that cold day
you called me—"Can you come?"
We took a taxi to the Right Bank, crossed
the river in its pewter gray, to the restaurant—
"you'll like it"—where we found
a table by the window, to watch boats pass,
ate boeuf bourguignon, and drank
good wine, to warm us.
You said, "one day we'll talk of it—death,
the loss of friends. But, not now.
Not today."

*

I go to lunch with friends, this Sunday
after news of your death,
I take you with me, your courage
in the face of everything: the Nazis
who took your bicycle
who killed your family,
even Eichmann in his glass box
with his robot talk.
You looked at it head on, the awful century,
tied on your turban—"look, I'm bald again!"
applied your lipstick, Chanel red,
and told me, life wins
on its own terms. Then, you left.
"Ciao-ciao! A bientot!
Je t'embrasse très fort."
And closed the door.